# Date Due

| | | |
|---|---|---|
| JUL 31 '97 | | |
| DEC 09 '98 | | |
| AUG 21 '07 | | |
| | | |
| | | |
| | | |
| | | |
| | | |
| | | |
| | | |
| | | |

D1361055

# FROG & TOAD WATCHING

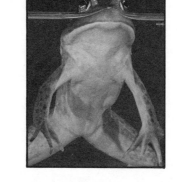

## David Webster

JULIAN MESSNER

PUBLISHED BY SIMON & SCHUSTER • NEW YORK

# To Duncan, and all other kids who like to catch frogs

Text copyright © 1986 by David Webster
Drawings copyright © 1986 by Tom LaPadula
All rights reserved including the right to reproduction in whole or in part in any form. Published by Julian Messner, A Division of Simon & Schuster, Inc., Simon & Schuster Building, Rockefeller Center, 1230 Avenue of the Americas, New York, New York 10020.

JULIAN MESSNER and colophon are trademarks of Simon & Schuster, Inc.

Designed by Lisa Hollander

Manufactured in the United States of America

10 9 8 7 6 5 4 3 2 1

Library of Congress Cataloging in Publication Data: Webster, David, 1930–  Frog and toad watching. Includes index. Summary: Describes the physical characteristics and life cycle of frogs and toads and discusses how to raise them in captivity.   1. Frogs—Juvenile literature. 2. Toads—Juvenile literature. 3. Frog culture—Juvenile literature. 4. Wildlife watching—Juvenile literature. [1. Frogs. 2. Toads] I. Title   QL668.E2W38  1986    597.8    86–7237

ISBN 0–671–60024–9 (Lib. bdg.)

Photo credits. P. 6 Henry B. Kane, Massachusetts Audubon Society; pp. 1, 9, 10, 12, 14, 44, 49, 59 Jerome Wexler; pp. 13, 16, 22, 69, 71 Mary Dickerson, American Museum of Natural History; p. 18 J. Kirschner, AMNH; pp. 23, 67 F. Overton, AMNH; pp. 24, 43, 73 Lemberger Company; p. 31 Bonnie Scott, The Brunswick Times; p. 41 AMNH; p. 47 R.E. Logan, AMNH; p. 62 Educational Development Center.

# CONTENTS

## ALSO BY DAVID WEBSTER

Spider Watching

# PREFACE

Have you ever caught a frog?

You know that a frog is good at hiding. Its mottled skin blends with plants and water. A frog watches you with huge eyes, ready to leap or swim away if you get too close. Often you do not spot a frog until it has escaped.

This book will tell you how to be a better frog catcher. The book also gives advice on how to keep a frog or toad as a pet. Raising tadpoles from frog eggs is another exciting project. There are pictures and descriptions of the common American frogs.

I hope my book will inspire you to learn more about the strange lives of our timid toads and friendly frogs.

David Webster

Toad catching caterpillar

# 1

# A CLOSE LOOK AT A FROG

Could you catch a fly with your tongue? Frogs and toads do it all the time. The tongue flicks out too fast for you to see. Scientists use high-speed cameras to study the action of the frog's lightning-fast tongue.

## Special Tongue

A frog's tongue is designed to catch flying insects and other prey. It is very different from your tongue. Instead of being short and fat, a frog's tongue is long and flexible. Even more important, it is attached in the front of the mouth. Stick out your tongue as far as you can. A lot of it is still inside your mouth. But a frog can flip out its tongue almost all the way.

There are other ways that a frog's tongue is suited for catching prey. The forks on the tip can wrap around an insect to hold it. The tongue also is coated with a sticky substance.

## What a Big Mouth!

Most frogs have big mouths, but they are not used for biting or chewing. Frogs swallow food whole. A big mouth allows the frog to gulp down large prey quickly before it can escape. Bullfrogs sometimes eat birds and mice as well as big insects. If a frog has trouble swallowing, it often uses its front feet to help stuff in the meal. Would you like to eat like a frog?

Most kinds of frogs have a row of very tiny teeth in the upper jaw. These are used to keep prey from getting away while it is being eaten.

## Bulging Eyes

Frogs and toads have eyes that stick out of their heads. Such eyes allow the animals to see in all directions at the same time. You will find it is hard to sneak up on a frog and catch it. The frog can see behind itself without turning its head.

When floating in the water, the frog can have its body hidden and still be able to see. The eyes stick up somewhat like the periscope on a submarine.

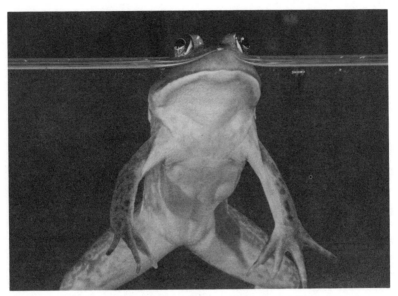

Frog underwater with eyes and nostrils above surface

Your eyes are protected by bony sockets. Think how many things would injure your eyes if they stuck out. Your forward-looking eyes are much better for judging distances, too.

A frog's upper eyelid is just a small fold of skin that cannot move much. The lower eyelid is more movable and partly transparent.

The frog's nostrils also are located on top of its flat head. With these air holes, the frog can breathe while still hidden underwater. Why does an alligator have nostrils, eyes, and ears on the top side of its head?

## Frog Ears

Frogs do have ears even though you may not have noticed them. They are the roundish spots just behind the eyes. The ear disk is called a *tympanum,* or eardrum.

You have eardrums, too, but you can't see them. Your outer ear narrows to a hole called the ear canal. The canal ends at your eardrum, which is about a quarter of an inch across. Sounds make the eardrum *vibrate,* or move back and forth quickly.

Even when underwater, a frog can hear sounds made in the air. Noises made by other animals alert the frog to possible danger. At mating time, female frogs are attracted by the croaking of male frogs.

Male bullfrog with tympanum larger than eye

Female with smaller tympanum

10

The size of the eardrum tells whether a bullfrog is male or female. A male bullfrog's eardrum is larger than the female's. You can see that in the photographs.

## Camouflaged Skin

One way frogs avoid being eaten is by hiding. It is harder for an enemy to find a frog that is colored the same as the place where it lives. The green skin of some tree frogs matches the color of leaves. A bullfrog's skin has splotches of dark green and brown, the same colors as the bottom of a pond.

The arum frog of South Africa is ivory colored. It hides in lily flowers of the same color. Then it catches insects that are attracted by the flower's perfume.

Usually a frog's underside is a lighter color. When seen in the water from below, its belly has the same color as the sunlit water. A hungry fish might not notice a tasty frog floating on the surface.

Some frogs can change the color of their skin to blend with different backgrounds. It may take several days for this to happen.

Coloration that helps animals hide is called *camouflage*. Hunters wear camouflaged clothing so they can hide from animals.

# Powerful Legs

One of the frog's best protections is its superior jumping ability. Many frogs rarely venture more than a few feet away from a pond. If threatened, the frog can make one big leap into the safe water.

**Bullfrog diving into water**

The hind legs of a frog are built perfectly for jumping. The legs look fat because of the large muscles. When the hind leg is stretched out, it is longer than the rest of the frog's body. The long hind foot gives the frog an extra push. The ankle joints are very flexible. When sitting, the frog's toes almost touch its knees. Can you do this?

Scientists have studied how a bullfrog jumps. They used a camera that took twenty pictures in a second. When the frog started to jump, its eyes were lowered into its head. Then the bullfrog pulled in its forelegs and stretched its hind legs straight out. Just before hitting the water, the frog raised its forelegs over its head. This is how people dive.

Bullfrogs are the champion jumpers of the frog world. The world's record is said to be a distance of over sixteen feet for three jumps in a row.

## Webbed Feet

Have you ever been swimming with flippers? You know how much faster you can go with

**Webbed hind foot of bullfrog**

swim fins. Navy frogmen and scuba divers use flippers while working underwater.

Swim fins for people were copied from frog feet. There is a thin skin stretched between the five toes of a frog's hind foot. This webbing gives the frog extra speed for swimming. Frogs that live mostly on land have smaller amounts of webbing.

## Slippery Skin

The frog's skin is good for swimming, too. The skin of most animals is covered by hair, feathers, or scales. The smooth skin of a frog helps it to glide through the water. Mucous glands produce a slimy liquid that makes the skin slippery.

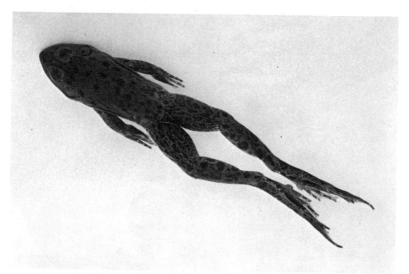

**Torpedo shape of swimming bullfrog**

You will find that frogs often escape capture by slipping out of your hands.

A frog's body is shaped like a torpedo: round with a pointed head. It has no fur or outside ears to drag in the water. By folding in its forelegs, the frog becomes even more streamlined.

## Toes with Sticky Disks

Webbed feet would not be of much value to tree frogs. Climbers need a different kind of foot.

Tree frogs have a round disk on the tip of each toe. These little sticky disks enable the frogs to cling to slippery surfaces. It is easy for tree frogs to climb trees and plant stems. They can even hang underneath a leaf.

## Adaption

The bodies of different animals are *adapted*, or suited, to their own way of life. Animals that eat flesh need sharp fangs, while grass eaters have rough molars for chewing. The quick tongue and big mouth of a frog is best for its diet of live insects and other small animals.

Animals also have different means to avoid being eaten by other creatures. How do skunks, rattlesnakes, and deer protect themselves? A frog hides from enemies. Its camouflaged body

**Suction disks on toes of tree frog**

can float motionless in the water; only the nostrils and bulging eyes break the surface.

An animal's legs are adapted to a certain method of movement. Horses have long legs for running. Moles dig tunnels with shovellike front feet. How are a frog's legs designed for jumping and swimming? Why are tree frogs' feet different from the feet of pond frogs?

16

# 2

# TOADS AND OTHER AMPHIBIANS

In the United States it usually is easy to tell a frog from a toad. Instead of a smooth, slick skin, toads have bumpy skin. Toads are fatter and less streamlined. With their shorter hind legs, they move by hopping rather than jumping. They spend much of their time on land, usually in moist areas.

## Dict

Toads eat the same food as frogs: live insects and other small animals. Their tongues can flick out as fast and as far as frogs' tongues. Toads have big mouths, but no teeth on either the top or bottom jaw.

American toad

## Poison Glands

Toads can secrete a weak poison from their skin. It comes from the *parotid glands,* the large swellings behind each eye, just above the eardrum. When threatened, the toad releases a toxic liquid from the glands. The poison has a very foul taste. A dog will not hold a toad in its mouth for more than a few seconds. The poison makes the attacking animal feel sick.

The bodies of most toads are covered with bumpy warts of various colors. The warts contain glands that secrete substances to keep the toad's skin moist so its body does not dry out.

Some people think you can get warts on your hands by touching a toad. This is not true. Do not be afraid to handle toads. It is a good idea, though, to wash your hands after handling any animal, especially before you eat.

## Other Defenses

In contrast to many brightly colored frogs, toads are mostly dull brown. They look like lumps of dirt. The camouflaged toad is even harder to notice when it remains motionless.

Toads are good diggers. Their hind feet are hardened, and serve as little shovels. The inner toe sticks out to the side like a spur.

Toads dig burrows under the edge of a stone or in soft garden soil. The toad makes its burrow and enters it at the same time—backwards. If an enemy comes, the toad backs in deeper until the soil caves in on the toad's head.

When attacked, a toad sometimes "plays dead." It lies on its back for many minutes without moving. Even the toad's breathing seems to stop. Then suddenly it rolls over and is ready for action.

Playing dead often saves the toad from injury or death. Animals that feed upon live toads seem to relate motion to life. When it sees a motionless creature, the attacking animal pays no attention to it.

## Hopping and Swimming

Toads are not good jumpers. Most can hop only short distances and some just walk.

Toads can swim and may spend several spring months in ponds. Later, many toads travel far from water. Some choose cool, moist places in the woods or around a flower garden. Desert toads burrow underground when their breeding ponds dry up. They do not wander around a dry desert.

Toads are *nocturnal*. Nocturnal animals are active at night rather than during the day. Toads sleep most of the day. When the air cools after dark, they leave their shaded burrows in search of food. Toads are always hungry, and eat many insects every evening.

# Amphibians

Toads and frogs are *amphibians*. The word "amphibian" comes from Greek words meaning "living a double life." Most frogs and toads begin their life as eggs laid in water. The eggs develop and hatch into tadpoles. The tadpoles live in water and breathe with gills as fish do. Later they change into frogs that breathe air. The "double life" of an amphibian is its tadpole stage in water and its adult stage on land breathing air.

Many animals spend part of their time in the water. Seals, ducks, and some turtles live in ponds or the sea. None of these animals is an amphibian, however. Baby seals, baby ducks, and baby turtles always breathe air; they have no tadpole stage.

# Salamanders

Salamanders are also amphibians. Unlike frogs and toads, adult salamanders are slender and have tails. Their skin is moist and slimy. All salamanders need moisture in order to stay alive. Some kinds, including all the larger ones, live in the water. Salamanders hide by day and move about during the night. Their bodies can replace lost parts, such as the tail and legs.

**Spotted salamander**

The spotted salamander is one of the most common kinds in North America. It is about six inches long and has yellow spots on dark skin.

The giant salamander of Japan grows to be five feet long.

Newts are salamanders with rough skin. Almost all newts live in the water.

# Reptiles

Amphibians are not the same as reptiles. Most people do not know the difference. There are four main kinds of reptiles: snakes, turtles, crocodiles, and lizards.

Most reptiles are covered by scales or plates, and their toes have claws. Most amphibians have no scales or claws. Reptiles lay eggs or give birth to living young. Reptile eggs have shells and are laid on land. Most amphibians lay eggs without shells in water. Baby reptiles look like their parents, while the tadpoles of amphibians do not.

## Eggs and Tadpoles_____

The eggs amphibians lay in water are covered with jelly and may be laid in clumps or singly. Toad eggs look like long strings of beads. Most kinds of frogs lay more than a hundred eggs and some lay thousands.

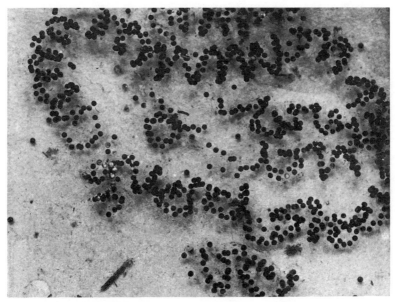

**Strings of toad eggs**

Amphibians can lay many eggs because the eggs are so small. Since reptile eggs are larger, most turtles and lizards lay less than thirty eggs at one time. Reptile eggs must have enough nourishment for the babies to reach full development before hatching.

Toad eggs in warm water often hatch in only three or four days. Frog eggs take longer, usually more than a week.

Just after hatching, tadpoles of different amphibians look the same. Differences can be noticed only as the tadpoles grow larger. Tadpoles of frogs and toads have outside gills for only a

Tadpoles

few days; salamanders have external gills for a long time. The front legs of salamander tadpoles grow faster. However, the hind legs of frogs and toad tadpoles develop first.

Different tadpoles have different eating habits, too. Salamander tadpoles hunt tiny water animals. Most frog and toad tadpoles eat only plant matter.

Toad tadpoles turn into adults quite quickly. The young toad is often ready to leave the water in six weeks. Frogs require most of the summer to develop, and the bullfrog often takes several years.

# Coldblooded

All amphibians and reptiles are coldblooded. Coldblooded animals do not produce heat inside their bodies. They are usually about the same temperature as the air or water around them. When the water is cold, a frog is cold. Frogs can warm up by basking in the sun. On a very hot day, a frog's body can be warmer than yours.

Birds and mammals—including people—are *warmblooded*. Unless you are ill, your body temperature is always the same: about 98° F. or 37° C. Food is "burned" inside your body to make heat.

# The First Voices on Earth

In the beginning, there were no animals living on land. Life began in oceans with small, soft-bodied animals. Animals with backbones developed much later.

All fishes had gills to breathe oxygen dissolved in the water. After a long time, a new kind of fish appeared. It had lungs for breathing air. A lungfish could live for a while out of water and could crawl along on its front fins. Perhaps it could travel to a new pond when its old one dried up.

As time passed, the fins of some fish became better adapted for walking. These animals with legs were the early amphibians, appearing about 350 million years ago. There were insects on the earth at that time. But amphibians were the first animals with backbones to inhabit the dry land.

Amphibians have never lost their connection with the water from which they evolved. Almost all frogs and toads return to the water each year for mating and egg-laying.

Visit a pond some evening in the spring. You may hear the musical croaking of unseen frogs and toads. Scientists believe that these were the first voices on earth!

# 3

# GO ON A
# FROG
# HUNT

Some toads and frogs make good pets. They do not bark, bite, or need big cages. Maybe you can catch a frog in a swamp or pond. Toads can often be found in the woods and around the yard.

Before going on a frog hunt, you should get a net and a carrying container.

## Nets

Nets used for catching water animals are called dip nets. They look like butterfly nets except the netting is stronger. You could buy a dip net from one of the science supply companies listed in the back of the book.

You can make a dip net yourself from a large kitchen strainer and a pole. The "ears" on the strainer should be cut off or bent out of the way. Then the rim should be bent into a triangular shape.

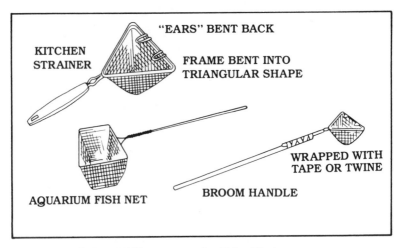

**How to Make a Homemade Dip Net**

A fish net could be used in place of the strainer. Pet stores sell nets for aquarium fish. A net for frogs should be large, at least six inches across the front. Sport stores have larger nets for fishing.

A dip net needs a long pole. The handle cut from an old broom is plenty strong enough. The net must be attached firmly to the pole with twine or plastic electrical tape. Use plenty of it so the net does not come off when used.

## Containers

A plastic or glass container can be used for carrying a frog. Many foods come in large plastic containers with snap tops. You should cut some small holes in the top with a paring knife. If you use a glass jar, punch holes in the screw cap

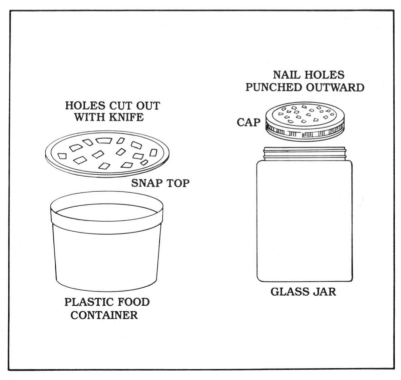

**Plastic and Glass Containers**

with a hammer and nail. Make the holes so the jagged points are outside, since a frog could be injured by sharp metal.

## Where to Look

Frogs are most common in swamps and small ponds. Frogs often float in the shallow water around the edges of the pond. On warm days they may climb out of the water and sit in the weeds on the bank.

Frogs come out of hibernation when the water warms up in the spring. Even in the summer they are harder to find when the weather is cool.

## How to Catch a Frog

To catch a frog, you need sharp eyes and quick hands. Of course, the frog will try not to get caught. You should try to see it before it sees you. And you must move your net quickly, before the frog's powerful legs can launch its body for an escape.

Walk slowly and quietly around the edge of the pond. Look carefully at the area five to ten feet ahead of you. If you see a frog, get your net ready. Try to get the net between the frog and the open water. Then push down the net as hard as you can. "Missed again!"

**Huge bullfrog caught in Maine by Tom Cloutier**

When you do catch a frog, carry it home in your container. The frog must be kept moist. Add some wet moss or damp leaves to the container, and keep it out of the sun.

## Spring Peepers

In many parts of the United States, peepers announce the coming of spring with their loud voices in the dark. Peepers prefer swampy areas with marsh plants rather than open pond water.

To catch spring peepers, you must wade into the swamp after dark. Be sure your parents know where you are going. You will need a flashlight and a small jar. The peepers will stop peeping as you move through the water. Stop and remain quiet, and they should start singing again. Shine the flashlight in the direction of the closest call. The light will reflect from the frog's eyes and puffed-up throat. Try to catch one of the little frogs with your hands or the jar.

## Toads

A toad is easy to catch if you find one. Usually a toad is found by chance, however. You just happen to see one as you are walking through the woods or playing in your yard. Since toads like to burrow in soft earth, you could try looking in a cultivated garden or farmer's field. Remember, toads are most active in the late afternoon and at night.

Live toads and frogs can be bought from science supply companies. You could request a catalog from one of the companies listed at the end of this book.

## Frog Cage

Amphibians have the same basic needs as you: food, water, air, and shelter. A glass aquarium makes the best cage for amphibians. A ten-gallon tank is big enough for two or three frogs or toads. A bullfrog needs a larger tank so it will not injure itself by banging into the sides and top. Large bullfrogs do not make good pets.

A frog cage will need a cage cover so the frog cannot hop out. Do not use a glass top; it would block fresh air movement. Coarse screening, called hardware cloth, is best. The screening can be bent down over the ends of the tank or stapled to a wooden frame.

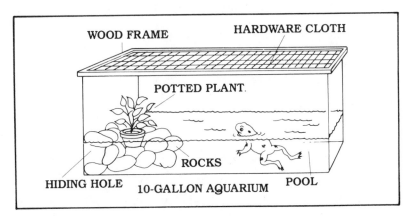

Frog Cage Design

Water is very important for all amphibians. Frogs and toads do not drink with their mouths. Instead, moisture is absorbed through the skin. An amphibian will die if it is kept in dry air for even a short time.

The frog must have a way to get out of the water. A small island of rocks or bricks can be built at one end of an aquarium partly filled with water. You could include a few potted plants or weeds in the island. Loose soil should not be put in since it will make the water muddy. It is very important to change the water if it does get dirty.

The frog will be more content if it has a place to hide. You could arrange the rocks to make a small cave. Or a piece of bark or wood could be propped up in a corner.

The temperature inside the cage should be controlled. Frogs and toads will not eat well if they are too cool. Too much heat will kill amphibians, so keep the cage out of the sun.

## Toad Cage

An aquarium for toads should have an area of damp, but not wet, soil. The toad can dig in the dirt and hide. Sprinkle a little water on the dirt every day to keep it moist. A cover over part of the tank helps to keep the soil from drying out.

Put in a piece of wood or bark for the toad to burrow under. You could plant some moss in part of the tank, but the toad may dig it up.

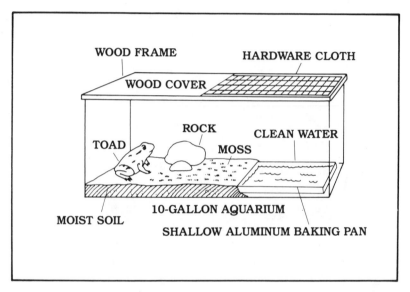

Toad Cage Design

Bury a pan for water in the soil so the toad will have a place to soak. The water may have to be changed daily.

# Feeding

Amphibians in captivity often are not good eaters. It is not unusual for a frog or toad to starve to death even when there is plenty of food in the cage.

Caged toads are better eaters than are frogs. Once a toad was fed houseflies one at a time, and it ate eighty-six in ten minutes.

Frogs and toads will eat only insects that are alive. Insects that crawl or walk are easier for the animal to catch than are those that fly. Perhaps you can find some ants, beetles, caterpillars, worms, or spiders. Many pet stores sell live mealworms and crickets. Any of these will make good food for your frog or toad.

You might be able to trick your frog or toad into eating a bit of meat. Attach a thread loosely to a small piece of hotdog or bologna and dangle it in front of the amphibian's head.

If your frog or toad does not eat, you should let it go. Try to release the amphibian in the same place it was found. Then you can find another frog or toad for your cage.

## Observations

You can learn a lot by watching carefully what your pet toad or frog does. Below are some suggestions for observations and experiments. Maybe you can think of other things yourself. Remember not to do anything that would cause the animal to suffer. Toads and frogs have tender skin, so they should be handled as little as possible.

## Catching Insects

Watch how your frog or toad hunts. Can you see its tongue when an insect is caught? Does the frog or toad ever miss? How are the forelegs used for eating?

## Swallowing

Watch the eyes of your pet when it swallows. You should see the eyes sink down into the skull. The eyes push into the roof of the mouth and help the frog or toad to swallow food.

## Toad Taming

Scientists think that toads are smarter than frogs. For this reason, they can be tamed more easily. Pick up your toad for a few minutes each day. It may learn to sit quietly in your hand.

Always feed the toad at the same place and at the same time of day. Does the toad soon learn to be waiting for its food? Can you teach your toad to take food from your fingers without waiting?

## Breath Holding

How long can your frog hold its breath? When a new frog is put into the tank, it may spend a lot of time trying to hide underwater. Use a watch to measure how long it stays down.

### Watching Outdoor Activity

Give your frog or toad some exercise outside. How far can your frog jump? Will a toad hide by burrowing into the soil? From how far away do you think your pet can see you? Try waving your arms around and see if it reacts.

### Observing Nighttime Activity

What do you think your toad or frog does all night? After the lights have been out awhile, sneak over to the tank with a flashlight. Can you catch the animal sleeping? Cover the flashlight lens with red cellophane. In the dim red light you can see the frog or toad behave as it does at night.

# LIFE CYCLE

Every animal has a *life cycle*. The cycle goes on and on forever, unless the animal becomes extinct. The stages of the life cycle of frogs and toads are: egg, tadpole, and adult.

**Frog Life Cycle**

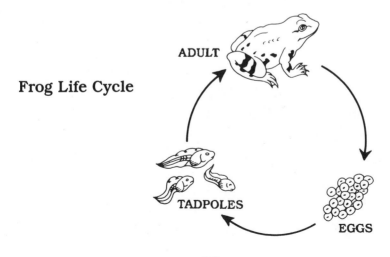

ADULT

TADPOLES

EGGS

The frogs and toads that have survived the northern winter come out of their deep sleep in the early spring. Guided by instinct, the amphibians find ponds and swamps soon after the ice has melted. Some toads, which live far from water, travel long distances. Many amphibians return to the same bodies of water in which they were born years before.

## The Noisy Chorus

Once the frogs are in the water, the singing begins. Each kind of frog has a different voice. The bullfrog makes a low, rumbly sound. Some people think the peepers' song sounds like distant sleigh bells. The pig frog is named for its grunting voice. A cricket frog chirps like a cricket, and the groans of a Florida gopher frog sound like a person snoring. Many toads have pretty, birdlike voices.

Male frogs and toads have louder voices. Females have either weak voices or none at all.

Even though frogs and toads are small creatures, they have very loud voices. What is even more surprising, they sing with their mouths closed!

# How Frogs Sing_____

A frog keeps its mouth and nostrils closed when singing. It pumps air back and forth from the lungs to the mouth. The air passes over the vocal cords, which vibrate to cause sound.

**Singing tree frog**

A singing frog looks like someone blowing bubble gum. This is because the frog has a pouch of thin skin under its throat. The pouch stretches like a balloon when air is forced up from the lungs. The inflated throat sac makes the croaking louder. Some kinds of frogs have a single pouch. Other kinds have two, one on each side going all the way to the base of the foreleg.

Bullfrogs and some other frogs even sing underwater. The next time you go swimming, see if you can do this.

## Distress Call

Frogs make another sort of noise: a distress call. This is a short, startled scream made with the mouth wide open. When a frog out of water is scared, it makes the scream as it leaps back in. Frogs also scream when caught by a raccoon or snake. The strange sound may scare the attacker enough to make it drop the frog.

## Mating

Frogs and toads do not sing because they are happy. Males use their voices to attract females for mating. Mating is a male and female frog coming together to make eggs. The female produces the eggs. But the eggs will not hatch unless they are fertilized with sperm from the male frog. The male and female frog must be the same kind in order to mate.

Each kind of frog has its own special call. Female bullfrogs recognize the voices of male bullfrogs. The female swims toward a male bullfrog, but ignores frogs with different voices.

Before mating, the smaller male frog holds on to the back of a female with his front feet. This is known as *clasping*. During breeding season, male frogs and toads develop spiny swellings on their front feet. The swellings help the male keep a firm grip on the slippery female.

Clasping leopard frogs

The female carries the male around until her eggs are ready. She can hop and swim and feed with the male on her back. The clasping can last from a few hours to several weeks. It usually ends as soon as the female finds a good place to lay her eggs.

Mating occurs in the water. The female lays her eggs while the male releases his sperm over them. The sperm fertilize the eggs, enabling them to develop.

# Egg Structure

Eggs of frogs and toads are not at all like the chicken eggs you eat for breakfast. Frog eggs have no shells and are much smaller. They are laid in a large mass surrounded by thick jelly.

The yolk of a frog egg is not yellow. Usually it is light in color on the bottom and dark on top. The dark color absorbs more heat from the sun, which helps the egg to develop into a tadpole. The yolks of pickerel frog eggs are so black that the whole egg mass looks dark.

Each yolk is enclosed by a membrane of clear jelly. The membranes are not visible when the eggs are first laid. They soon absorb water and

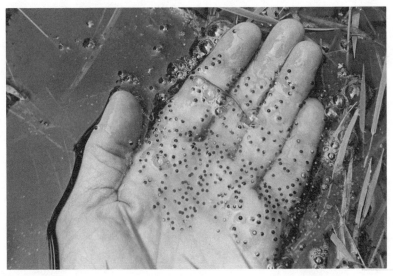

Frog eggs

swell up. Sometimes the egg mass becomes larger than the frog that laid it.

The jelly membranes insulate the eggs from the cool water. This keeps the yolks at a more constant temperature. The slippery jelly also makes it harder for the frog's enemies to eat the eggs.

The egg masses are often attached to water weeds, but some float on the surface of the water. Usually tree frog eggs are laid in smaller clusters. Toads lay eggs in long strings.

## Number and Size of Eggs

Most toads and frogs lay many eggs all at once. A spring peeper lays several hundred, and a bullfrog might deposit twelve thousand. Larger frogs do not always produce more eggs than smaller frogs.

The size of the individual egg does not depend on the size of the frog or toad. A tiny frog can have eggs the size of your fingertip. Without the jelly, bullfrog eggs are not much larger than a pinhead.

## Hatching

The time for hatching depends on the weather temperature. If it is warm, some kinds of toad eggs hatch in two days. They would take two to three weeks in colder weather.

At first, the shape of the egg yolk changes from round to a lopsided oval. Then the black speck grows a head, gills, and pointed tail. A dark groove marks the developing backbone. Finally, the tiny tadpole starts to wiggle.

It is difficult for the weak tadpole to escape from the egg jelly. The tadpole has a special gland on the tip of its nose. The gland gives off a secretion that softens and dissolves the jelly. After many hours of squirming, the tadpole finally breaks out. Its new life has begun.

## Baby Tadpoles

Many dangers lurk in the tadpole's underwater world. Tadpoles are eaten by leeches, water beetles, fish, wading birds, snakes, and frogs. Hundreds of tadpoles are killed for every one that lives long enough to turn into a frog.

The newborn tadpole looks like a little stick. Its head and tail are almost too small to see. It has no eyes or mouth. The tadpole rests motionless on the bottom of the pond. It seems worn out after its struggle to hatch.

Soon the tadpole begins to move about. It uses its tail for swimming because tadpoles have no other fins. Tadpoles sink to the bottom when they stop swimming. They have no air bladder as fish have for floating. The tadpole can hold on to water plants with its mouth or with a sucker located under its head.

Tiny branches sprout from either side of the tadpole's head. These are the external gills. The gills absorb oxygen that is dissolved in the water.

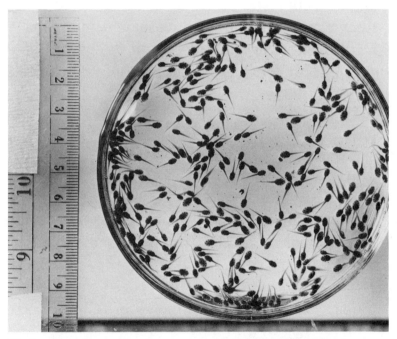

**Tadpoles less than one week after hatching**

After a few days, the tadpole's eyes and mouth form. The mouth is round with a horny beak inside. Its lips are covered with rows of tiny, rasping teeth.

Tadpoles are always eating or looking for food. Algae is scraped from rocks and larger plants with their rough lips. They also feed upon decaying plants. With so much food, the tadpole grows quickly. Its body begins to get fat and the tail becomes stronger.

After a few weeks, the outside gills slowly disappear. They are replaced by new ones growing just under the skin. Now the tadpole must gulp water like a fish. The water in the mouth is forced back over the gills and flows out the *spiracle*. The spiracle is a small hole on the left side of the body.

## Inside Changes

Big changes take place inside the tadpole. For breathing, a frog needs lungs. Lungs develop in a tadpole while it is still using gills to breathe. As the tadpole changes from using gills to using lungs, it pops to the surface to gulp breaths of air.

The diet of frogs and tadpoles is different, too. A tadpole is a plant eater, and must have a long intestine. Animals that eat other animals have shorter intestines. So the tadpole's intestines shorten in preparation for the frog's animal diet. At the same time, the tadpole's little mouth begins to look more like the gaping mouth of a frog.

# Legs

The hind legs grow first. Bulges form at the base of the tail. One hind leg breaks out of the skin, followed by the second one. Later the left front leg pops out through the gill hole. Usually the right front leg appears last.

When the hind legs grow larger, the tadpole begins to use them for swimming. At about the same time, the tadpole stops eating. The changing intestines prevent it from digesting food. Instead, the tadpole gets energy from its tail as it is absorbed into the body.

Frog with tail almost absorbed

## A Frog at Last

The tadpole soon looks almost like a frog. Its legs strengthen and the eyes bulge out more and more. The tail becomes a mere stub and then disappears entirely. The tadpole is finally a frog!

Most tadpoles take about two months to develop into frogs. In the north, bullfrog tadpoles require two to three years to become adults. In the south, where the water is warmer, bullfrogs develop in a year.

Some toad tadpoles can change into an adult in several weeks. Quick development is important because many toads live where water is scarce. The small pools where toads lay eggs often dry up quickly.

## Frog Food

Frogs and tadpoles are alike in at least one way: both are big eaters. All summer, frogs and toads spend much time hunting for food. Little frogs eat only small insects and spiders. Bullfrogs are big enough to gulp down baby turtles, young birds, crayfish, and snakes. Sometimes a young frog will try to eat an insect much too big for its mouth.

Good eyesight is needed to catch flying and swimming prey. Frogs and toads see things best that are a few feet away. Distant vision is not important, since an amphibian does not chase its prey. Even when an insect is close enough to be seen, it is not recognized as food unless it is moving.

## Estivation

Amphibians cannot live long in hot, dry conditions. During hot sunny days, frogs and toads like to hide in places that are dark and moist, or in ponds and puddles.

Toads have a special way to escape long periods of dry weather. They become inactive after digging deep into the ground where it is moist. This is called *estivation.*

Frogs and toads need a lot of water, but they cannot drink it. Instead, water is absorbed through their skin. Toads often get water by sitting in puddles after a rainstorm.

## Shedding Skin

Frogs and toads shed their skins quite often. Some shed every few days.

When shedding, the frog yawns and stretches and wiggles to make its skin split down the back. Then the frog pulls off the old skin with its mouth and front feet. It looks like someone taking off a sweatshirt. Usually the discarded skin is eaten by its owner.

## Enemies

Frogs and toads have many enemies. Stalking herons try to stab frogs with their sharp beaks. Carnivorous land animals, such as bobcats, raccoons, and opossums use their sharp fangs to seize toads and frogs. Underwater attacks on frogs come from fish and turtles. Big frogs even eat smaller frogs.

Humans are the frogs' worst enemy. Frogs' legs are a favorite food of many people, especially in China and France. Many more frogs lose their homes and lives when land is developed for houses, factories, and farms.

With so many enemies, few frogs die of old age. Most frogs are killed before they have lived a year. A lucky few grow to be ten years old. Frogs and toads kept as pets or in zoos have lived for twenty-five years.

## Hibernation

The approach of winter is signaled by shorter days and cooler temperatures. Frogs and toads in the north spend the winter in *hibernation*. Some frogs burrow into the mud on the bottom of ponds. Others hide on land under rocks, dead leaves, or rotten logs. Here the amphibians stay for many months in a deep sleep.

A frog in hibernation does not eat or move. Its heart beats much more slowly. The frog's body becomes as cold as the mud around it. The frog will die if its body temperature goes much below freezing.

In the spring, the ice melts and the frost thaws from the soil. Slowly frogs and toads awaken from hibernation. Mating time has come again. The cycle of life continues.

# 5

# RAISE SOME TADPOLES

It is pretty easy to raise tadpoles. Watching tadpoles grow is the best way to learn how they turn into frogs or toads.

## Where to Get Eggs

Amphibian eggs often can be found in the shallow water of a small pond or swampy area. Any pond with grass edges or cattails is a likely place to look. Wear old sneakers; you may have to wade out into the water. Take a covered container for carrying the eggs home.

An egg mass is very slippery, so you probably will not be able to pick it up with your hands.

Scoop it up in the container, along with some water. Try not to break the egg mass apart. Eggs not surrounded with jelly do not hatch as well.

Frogs and toads in the north usually mate and lay eggs in March and April. In the south, eggs are laid throughout the year, but mostly during the hotter months from April to August.

Amphibian eggs can also be purchased from science supply companies. The addresses of some companies are listed in the Appendix at the back of the book. Companies that breed frogs in the laboratory have eggs available from November into early June. Other companies, which sell eggs collected outside, can supply eggs only in the springtime.

Tadpoles are easier to find than eggs. Look for them as you walk along the shore of a pond. When you get close, the frightened tadpoles often swim out into the deeper water. Try to catch some with a kitchen strainer or aquarium dip net.

## Aquarium

A ten-gallon aquarium makes a good home for hatching eggs and raising tadpoles. A large glass jar also could be used. A plastic container is not as good if you cannot see through the sides.

# Water

Of course, the best water for tadpoles comes from a swamp or pond. Gallon milk containers can be used to transport the water to your tank. There should be enough water to float the eggs.

Water from the faucet can be used instead of pond water. Unless your house has its own well, your water will contain chemicals. Chlorine is added to kill harmful bacteria. To remove the chlorine, just let the water sit in the aquarium for several days before adding the eggs. The poisonous gases disappear into the air.

Another source of water is bottled spring water sold in supermarkets. The minerals in spring water help the tadpoles grow. Water in ponds has minerals that have come from the soil.

# Temperature

The water in the aquarium should be kept at the proper temperature. Eggs and tadpoles will not develop properly if the water is too cold. The water should not be too hot, either. A temperature of 70° F. is best, but 60–65° F. is safe.

The tank should not be placed in the sun. It is a good idea to have a thermometer in the water to make sure it is the proper temperature.

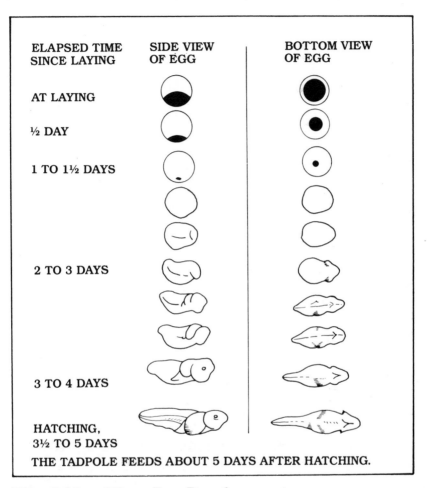

| ELAPSED TIME SINCE LAYING | SIDE VIEW OF EGG | BOTTOM VIEW OF EGG |
|---|---|---|
| AT LAYING | | |
| ½ DAY | | |
| 1 TO 1½ DAYS | | |
| 2 TO 3 DAYS | | |
| 3 TO 4 DAYS | | |
| HATCHING, 3½ TO 5 DAYS | | |

THE TADPOLE FEEDS ABOUT 5 DAYS AFTER HATCHING.

Timetable of Frog Egg Development

# Hatching

Once the eggs are placed in the aquarium, you have nothing to do but watch. Look at them several times each day. You might want to make drawings so you can remember how the eggs change.

How to use a magnifying glass: Hold the glass close to your eye. Move the object back and forth to bring it into focus.

A magnifying glass will help you see details in the developing eggs. Practice using the magnifying glass by looking at your fingernail. Hold the lens of the magnifier as close to your eye as you can. Then move your finger back and forth until it is in clear focus.

# Baby Tadpoles

The eggs should hatch in less than a week. Some of the yolks may stay white and not change shape. These are eggs that may not have been fertilized by sperm from the male; they will never hatch. The remaining jelly and unhatched eggs should be removed before they start to rot.

Tadpoles require more space in the water than

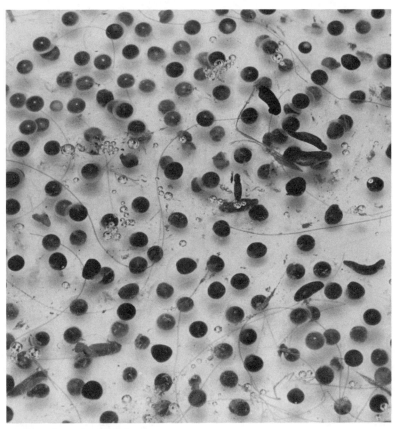

Tadpoles hatching

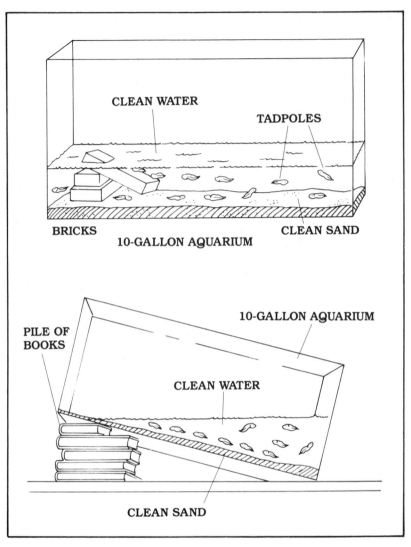

**Tadpole Tanks**

the eggs needed. If the tadpoles are crowded, all may die. For each tadpole, you should have a pint of water. You can keep about eight tadpoles for each gallon of water in the tank.

Extra tadpoles should be removed from the tank with an aquarium net or strainer. It would be kind to release the unneeded tadpoles in a pond.

Tadpoles like to rest on the bottom in shallow water. There are several ways to create a shallow-water zone in the tank. A slope can be made by piling up several bricks. Or the entire tank can be tipped by putting books under one end. Also, some sand could be added to make a more natural bottom.

Mark the side of the tank so you can remember the height of the water. Add more every few days as the water evaporates. All the water should be changed if it becomes cloudy or begins to smell.

## Feeding

Tadpoles do not eat until they are about a week old. After this time, they must have food in order to grow. Tadpoles can live for a week or so without eating.

The best food for tadpoles is algae, a microscopic plant that grows in pond water. You can collect algae from a pond. Look for green scummy growths. Gather some pond plants and slimy rocks from the bottom.

Put all the algae and underwater plants in

the aquarium at the same time. Once started, the algae should continue to grow faster than the tadpoles eat it.

**Tadpole with legs**

Many kinds of water plants can be bought in pet stores. The tadpoles will feed on rotten vegetation from dead leaves.

If you cannot get algae, you can feed your tadpoles a bit of crushed dog food. Cooked spinach or lettuce leaves also can be used. Boil the leaves until they become limp and mushy.

Add only a *tiny bit* of food twice a week. Uneaten food will decay and foul the water. The bacteria that cause decay use up the oxygen in the water, which the tadpoles need. Cloudy water is a sign of bacteria. Change the water immediately if this happens.

Some science supply companies sell special tadpole food.

## On to Frogs

Tadpoles grow fast when conditions are right. You might try to draw some pictures of tadpoles in different stages. You could keep track of the development by writing in a notebook when each stage is reached.

| Stage | Day |
|---|---|
| Tadpole hatches | |
| First seen swimming | |
| Gills appear | |
| Fat body develops | |
| Gills disappear | |
| Length exceeds 2 cm. | |
| Hind legs appear | |
| Front legs appear | |
| Hind legs used for swimming | |
| Tail begins to shorten | |
| Gulps air at surface | |
| Sits partly out of water | |
| Becomes a frog | |

Even the best of care will not assure success in raising frogs. Tadpoles often die when kept in captivity. If your tadpoles grow weak, they should be returned to a pond. As you dump the tadpoles back, be sure to thank them for teaching you so much about their amazing life cycle.

# COMMON FROGS IN THE UNITED STATES

There are some 2,500 different kinds of frogs and toads in the world. Probably the most familiar frogs in the United States are the bullfrog, spring peeper, pickerel frog, and leopard frog. Do you know any other kinds of frogs? Which one is your favorite?

## Spring Peeper

One of the best known frogs is the spring peeper, even though very few people ever see them. Their loud chorus of chirping voices is the first sign of spring in many parts of the eastern United States.

The scientific name of the peeper is *Hyla crucifer*. The first name of all tree frogs is *Hyla*. *Crucifer* means "cross-bearing." That is because the spring peeper has a brown "X" on its back. Sometimes the mark looks more like an upside down "Y."

Spring peepers have brown or grayish green skin with bands of darker colors on the hind legs. The mottled colors blend with the pond plants to camouflage the frog. A peeper's skin can change to a lighter color on warm days.

Spring peepers have the toe pads found on most tree frogs. The pads are made sticky with a gluelike liquid secreted from glands within the toes. The special toes make it easy for a peeper to climb trees and slippery grass.

You may not have ever seen a frog as small as the peeper. It is only an inch long, or about as big as the end of your thumb. You would not expect a frog this small to have such a large voice.

When singing, the little frog clings to grass or twigs at the water's edge. With the yellow throat pouch puffed up, it looks almost twice as big.

In the north, peepers begin to peep with the first warm rain. They mate in the south from late November to March. After mating, the frogs leave the water and live in bushes or the bark of tree trunks.

## Cricket Frog

The cricket frog is a tree frog that cannot climb trees. Its toe pads are too tiny for climbing. It is found on the ground in open marshy areas. Unlike most frogs, this tree frog has a rough and warty skin.

Cricket frog

A cricket frog is a good swimmer and jumper. Upon sighting an insect, the frog catches it by leaping high into the air. Cricket frogs escape their enemies by making a series of giant hops in rapid order.

Cricket frogs might have been named for their small size or their cricketlike jumps. Probably, though, the name comes from their voice, which resembles the pleasant chirping of a cricket.

## Other Tree Frogs

Many other kinds of tree frogs live in North America. The green tree frog is dark green, but many turn yellow when calling. The power for its graceful leaps comes from long hind legs. Sometimes people see green tree frogs outside their windows at night. The frogs are searching for insects attracted by the lights inside.

Not all tree frogs have musical voices. The barking tree frog makes a barking noise from the treetops. The squirrel tree frog was named because of its squirrellike voice. Some people think the call of the Mexican tree frog sounds like an old car when the motor is being started.

The tiniest frog in North America is the little grass frog. It is only one-half inch long. The little grass frog's voice is so high and shrill that some people have trouble hearing it.

## Bullfrog

The bullfrog is famous because of its size. It is so big that bullfrog tadpoles in the North usually take two years to become adult frogs. The bullfrog's name has nothing to do with its size. Instead, the name refers to its deep croaking, perhaps like the bellowing of a distant bull.

The largest bullfrog ever found had a body that was eight inches in length. Most bullfrogs grow to be between three-and-one-half to six inches long.

**Male Southern bullfrog**

The bullfrog is one of many frogs that have the ability to change their skin color. Its back is normally olive green and marked with brown spots. In warm air, however, the skin may become light green without any spots. When emerging from hiding in deep water, a bullfrog can be almost black.

A bullfrog eats anything it can get in its mouth and swallow. In the water, it feeds on smaller frogs, crayfish, little fish, and baby turtles. The turtles' shells are dissolved by the bullfrog's strong digestive juices. Bullfrogs even eat such larger animals as birds, bats, snakes, and mice.

Bullfrogs are late in coming out of hibernation. Their deep, bass voices are often not heard until late May or early June. Bullfrogs prefer large ponds where they can find deep water as well as shallow. You might find one hiding under the leaves of water weeds.

## Green Frog

It is easy to confuse a large green frog with a small bullfrog. Both look alike and spend most of the time in the water. You can tell a green frog by the folds of skin that are on each side of the body.

Some green frogs may be more brown than green. A few have been found that are blue! Normal green color is a mixture of blue and yellow skin pigments. If the yellow pigment is missing, blue skin results.

Sometimes green frogs are called spring frogs because they are early to emerge from hibernation.

# Pickerel Frog

Pickerel frogs live out of the water more than in it. They do go to the water to lay eggs and to absorb water through their shiny skins. They spend the warm months in the grasses along brooks and in marshy meadows. Sometimes pickerel frogs are found in springs and shallow wells.

Female pickerel frog

Pickerel frogs have medium-sized bodies from two to three inches long. Their agile leaps make them hard to catch. You can tell a pickerel frog by the rows of squarish spots down its back. Also, the skin is bright yellow or orange on the hidden parts of the hind legs. When in bright light, the color of a young pickerel frog becomes a glistening gold.

Not many snakes will eat a pickerel frog. Their skin secretes a mild poison. It is safe for you to handle pickerel frogs, but wash your hands before touching your lips or eyes.

Do not put a pickerel frog in a cage with other kinds of frogs. Its poison could kill them.

## Leopard Frog

Leopard frogs are related to pickerel frogs. You can tell the difference by the spots; leopard frogs have round spots instead of square ones. Of course, the leopard frog was named because its skin patterns look so much like the spotted coat of a leopard.

Leopard frogs are beautifully colored. They are metallic green above and pearly white below. The spots are olive green or brown and are circled by a narrow yellow line. There are many variations in the colors and patterns of different leopard frogs.

**Northern leopard frog**

Leopard frogs spend a lot of time in tall grasses, often quite a distance from any ponds. For this reason, sometimes they are called grass frogs.

## Wood Frog

The wood frog appears to wear a "robber's mask." It has a dark patch extending backward from the eyes. The frog's brown and tan colors help it to hide in dead leaves. The skin color can change from dark to light in less than half an hour.

Wood frogs spend only a brief period in the water at breeding time. After this they wander off to moist wooded areas. They live in the eastern United States and quite far north in Canada and Alaska.

# APPENDIX

## Science Supply Companies

Carolina Biological Supply Co.
2700 York Road
Burlington, NC 27215
919-584-0381

Insect Lore Products
P.O. Box 1535
Shaffer, CA 93263
805-746-6047

Lemberger Co.
P.O. Box 482
Oshkosh, WI 54901
414-231-8410

Nasco Science
901 Janesville Road
Ft. Atkinson, WI 53538
414-563-2446

# INDEX

## About the Author————————

David Webster teaches elementary science at two schools in Massachusetts. He was a staff member of the elementary science study of the Education Development Center. Mr. Webster has written twelve science books, including *Spider Watching* and *Track Watching*. The author lives in Lincoln, Massachusetts, and spends summers on Bailey Island in Maine.